THE
GREAT
PHILOSOPHERS

Consulting Editors
Ray Monk and Frederic Raphael

Kenneth McLeish

....

ARISTOTLE

Aristotle's Poetics

PHŒNIX

A PHOENIX PAPERBACK

First published in Great Britain in 1998 by
Phoenix, a division of the Orion Publishing Group Ltd
Orion House
5 Upper Saint Martin's Lane
London, WC2H 9EA

A CIP catalogue record for this book is available
from the British Library

ISBN 0 753 80203 1

Typeset by Deltatype Ltd, Birkenhead, Merseyside

Printed in Great Britain by
Clays Ltd, St Ives plc

ARISTOTLE

Aristotle's Poetics

Note: All quotations are from Aristotle's *Poetics*. I have used the translation by the nineteenth-century scholar S. H. Butcher, modernizing and expanding it here and there to make the meaning clearer. Substantial editorial interventions are in square brackets. Numbers at the ends of sections refer to sections of Aristotle's original.

KMcL

KEY DATES

All the following dates are BC.

before 700	Homer
c.536	First-ever 'tragedy' performed in Athens
525	Aeschylus born
c.496	Sophocles born
c.485	Euripides born
480	Greeks destroy Persian fleet at battle of Salamis; Sophocles a boy dancer and singer in the victory-celebrations
472	Aeschylus' *Persians*
469	Socrates born
458	Aeschylus' *Oresteia*
456	Aeschylus died
c.450	Aristophanes born
441	Sophocles' *Antigone*
431	Euripides' *Medea*; Peloponnesian War begins between Athens, Sparta and their respective allies
c.429	Sophocles' *Oedipus Tyrannos*; Plato born
428	Euripides' *Hippolytos*
415	Euripides' *Women of Troy*
c.414	Euripides' *Iphigeneia in Tauris*
413	Euripides' *Elektra*
411	Aristophanes' *Lysistrata*
406	Euripides died; Sophocles led his chorus in mourning at the summer drama

ARISTOTLE

Aristotle was born in 384 BC in Stageira, some 55 km east of what is now Thessaloniki. His father was court physician to King Amyntas of Macedon, and Aristotle was given the standard aristocratic education of the time, culminating in a journey to Athens when he was seventeen, to study with Plato. He stayed there for twenty years, leaving only when Speusippos, Plato's successor, began giving the academic study of philosophy a mathematical bias that Aristotle (by all accounts no mathematician) found uncongenial. After a dozen years in northern Greece (seven of them spent as tutor to the future Alexander the Great), he returned to Athens in 335 BC and founded a teaching institution of his own, the Lyceum, which remained a centre of research and learning until it was closed by the Roman emperor Justinian 860 years later.

Aristotle and his followers believed that human curiosity was infinite, and that no subject was unworthy of systematic study. Aristotle himself left treatises on botany, ethics, history, literary composition, logic, metaphysics, meteorology, oratory, the physical world, political science, religion and zoology. In contrast to earlier Greek philosophers, including Plato, he placed less reliance on discussion and flashes of intellectual inspiration than on research and inductive logic. Each enquiry began with the exhaustive compilation of existing evidence, both physical – a quest whose range was restricted only by the non-existence of scientific instruments – and written. The material was then codified according to the principles of logic, and only when this work was completed did the researcher propose theories and conclusions of his own. The same method was applied to each subject of study, whether physical objects (such as stones or animals), human constructs (such as plays or systems of government) or abstractions (such as virtue or justice).

Aristotle's conclusions were never meant to be prescriptive; they were, rather, a summary of all evidence so far available, with conclusions drawn from it. In his view, new material and new evidence were constantly appearing, and theories should be modified to take account of them. His surviving works – about one-quarter of the total attributed to him – are not finished treatises so much as interim reports, often in the form of notes and containing accumulations and accretions of material made over many years. He can seem inconsistent and self-contradictory; no doubt if he had revised his work himself for publication, he would have attended to this problem. *Poetics*, for example, combines detailed description and analysis of practicalities (such as a lengthy typology of that standard but hardly major component of ancient tragedy, the recognition scene: see '*Anagnorisis* and *peripeteia*', page 31) with blunt assertions about intangibles (such as the half sentence outlining the function of tragedy: 'through pity and terror it effects the purgation of these emotions').

POETICS

I propose to discuss literary and dramatic composition.
I shall examine the essential qualities of the art itself and
of its various manifestations. I shall inquire into how
material should be organised to make a successful
literary work, into the number and nature of its constitu-
ent parts, and into all other relevant matters. And I shall
begin, naturally, with first principles. (1)

In the tenth book of his *Republic*, written in the 370s BC,
Plato launched an attack on the arts more ironical, mischie-
vous and provocative – we might say more 'Shavian' – than
anything else in his surviving work. He seems to have
wanted rather to twit the artistic community than to make
serious philosophical points (though that has never pre-
vented philosophers from taking him seriously). An artist,
he said, is 'third in line to the throne of truth', because (for
example) whereas God makes 'bed' and a carpenter makes
'a bed', an artist makes only the representation of a bed. We
may admire Homer and enjoy his descriptions of (say)
generalship or doctoring, but we would hardly go to him
for leadership in a real battle or healing in a real disease.
Artists, in particular dramatists, show 'distorted' characters
rather than 'true' ones: for example, when they let people
give open expression to emotions that we restrain in
ordinary life. The quarrel between philosophy and art is
that philosophy defines while art – 'a bitch growling and
snarling at its owner' – merely describes.

Plato ends his remarks by inviting anyone who loves the
arts to defend them on the grounds that they bring not just
pleasure but some kind of benefit to human life and

society; if this cannot be done, the arts will be banned from the ideal society. This challenge is in part taken up in Aristotle's *Poetics*. The book, which was first circulated in the 340s BC, some thirty years after Plato's attack, dealt with music, dance and the fine arts as well as with literature. Twenty-six short sections survive, about half the total. They deal with tragedy and epic (in Aristotle's day the principal forms of literary fiction); comedy is promised in the text, but missing.

Although *Poetics* is one of Aristotle's minor works, its fame and influence in later centuries far exceeded this position. Both in ancient Rome (where Horace and Longinus admired and extended Aristotle's arguments) and in the Renaissance and beyond, it was treated as a seminal text of aesthetic and dramatic criticism, and Aristotle's observations, mistaken views of them or reactions to those views influenced the discussion and practice of 'serious' Western drama for over two millennia.

THE FUNCTION OF TRAGEDY

Tragedy is the imitation of an action that is serious, complete, and of a certain magnitude; in language embellished with each kind of artistic ornament, the several kinds being found in separate parts of the play. In form it is action, not narrative. Through pity and terror it effects the purgation of these emotions. By 'language embellished' I mean language into which enter rhythm, harmony and song. By 'the several kinds being found in separate parts' I mean that some parts are rendered

> through the medium of verse alone, others again with
> the aid of song. (6)

It is fundamentally unGreek to attribute any specific didactic or therapeutic impulse to artistic creation in general or to any artist in particular. *Poetics* may talk of the 'purgation' of emotions, but this is the (possible) effect of tragedy rather than its intrinsic purpose. The activity of writing plays or epic poems is analogous less to that of (say) a priest who presides over the relationship between mortals and gods or a teacher who changes minds than to that of the artisan who makes a table. Carpenters need not agonize about the eventual function of the furniture they make: they know what it is before they start. So it is, in *Poetics* at least, with authors of literary fiction.

Greek moral 'teaching' was nothing like that of later Europe, with its Judaeo-Christian emphasis on scripture and on action learned from precedent. In Greek religion, only a few fringe cults (for example, Orphism) had sacred books. Custom and practice were not prescribed but were the result of an evolutionary process; they were reinforced by reference to myth-stories, selectively retold (and in some cases made up or revised *ad hoc*) to validate attitudes or behaviour. Like the anecdotes families tell about distant relatives, myths served to reinforce a continuum of group identity; they were capacious and protean; few contained imperatives for thought or action, in the way of Judaeo-Christian scriptural anecdote.

The idea that morality and ethics could be codified at all was recent even in Aristotle's day, and resulted less from an impulse to prescribe or preach than from the incessant question-asking and solution-proposing that were characteristic of early Greek philosophy. The enquiry was into the nature of virtue and its manifestations; whether an individual went on from such a quest to choose or reject virtuous behaviour was not the philosopher's prime concern. *Mimesis* (see page 12), the chief process of the arts, was a matter less of moral indoctrination than of the (selective) imitation of reality. This 'reality' need not be physical; emotions and thoughts could also be represented. Music could – indeed should – represent emotion. Dance could show not only what people did or had done to them, but what they were like. Sculpture, as well as showing what people looked like, could also represent the 'ideal' in such qualities as beauty or nobility. The literary arts made statements about human actions and motives and the behaviour of gods and other supernatural beings who impinged on the mortal world. Homer's poems, and in Aristotle's time the works of the great Athenian dramatists, were particularly admired for the diversity and acuity of such passages.

Clearly, such *mimesis* contains the possibility of moral effect, whether consciously intended by the artist or not. Aristotle's view is that our minds are endlessly curious, ceaselessly looking for explanations and connections. In real life a table or a written constitution can appeal not only because it is useful but because of the skill and elegance of its construction. Even things that do not appeal aesthetically can evoke such admiration: the range extends from vermin to master criminals. Our satisfaction consists not merely in observing, but in criticizing, evaluating, making comparisons. These activities produce pleasure, the chief purpose of all artistic activity. But the pleasure is not mindless. It involves intellectual and emotional engagement on the part of the spectators, and that engagement affects and alters them. (Not for nothing is theatre under the protection of Dionysos, god of change.) In Aristotle's thinking, willed change of this kind should always be for the better, not the worse, and hence the 'best' art in general, and the 'best' drama in particular, should tend towards the moral and ethical 'improvement' of the spectator. Art that morally degrades the spectator is worse even than art that has no moral function at all. The caricatured Aeschylus relates this point to tragedy in Aristophanes' *Frogs* (405 BC), saying that dramatists 'teach' adults as tutors teach children, and deploring the kind of moral examples that Euripides' characters offer to his audience. This is the nub of Plato's objection to the arts (on the grounds that fiction is morally inferior to fact) and the unstated but underlying theme of *Poetics* is that literary art, if created with propriety, dignity and excellence, can do, precisely, everything that Plato claims that it cannot.

The argument continues, both in academe and in the real world. As little as two decades ago, Plato's viewpoint was robustly echoed by the father of a British mathematical prodigy. In educating his daughter, this man said, he had forbidden her to read fiction of any kind, because it was frivolous and irrelevant. The implication that Aeschylus, Shakespeare, Goethe, Dickens, Dostoevsky and a host of others have nothing to tell us, nothing to teach us, hardly bears analysis. Aristotle might have claimed that culture is a single entity, an indivisible attribute of the human species, and that to exclude this or that aspect of it is to impoverish ourselves.

The fact remains, however, that the provision of examples is not the same as teaching. The 'lessons' of literature, in Aristotle's time no less than today, are oblique rather than direct and are not prescriptive; there is no more obligation on anyone to try, in daily life, to live up to the excellences or avoid the excesses depicted than there is to emulate the 'ideal' qualities represented by (say) such sculptors as Pheidias or Canova. This is the light in which all Aristotle's statements in *Poetics* should be taken. Tragedy is not dogmatic; the moral health of the audience is not its primary concern. It is a series of pictures, a repository of examples of how specific types of people reacted in specific circumstances. Its power – which may or may not include the power to change people – depends on each author's success at selecting and articulating what the audience is shown, and it is that selection and articulation with which *Poetics* mainly deals.

MIMESIS

All the arts – epic, tragedy, comedy, dithyrambic poetry, the music of the flute and of the lyre – have in common that they are kinds of imitation. They differ from one another in three respects: the means of imitation, the objects imitated and the different ways they imitate the same things.

Just as there are people who, by skill or experience, imitate and represent various objects by drawing them or describing them, so in all the arts above mentioned, imitation is produced by rhythm, language or melody, either singly or in combination. In the music of the flute and of the lyre, and in other, similar arts such as that of playing the shepherd's pipe, melody and rhythm are employed. In dance, rhythm is used alone without melody: dancing imitates character, emotion, and action by rhythmical movement. Other arts – dithyrambic poetry, sacred song, tragedy, comedy – use all three means above mentioned, namely, rhythm, melody and language. Sometimes these means are employed together, at other times separately.

The difference between one art-form and another is not in the fact of imitation, but in the means used to do it. (1)

The arts imitate people doing things. Since 'goodness' and 'badness' are the distinguishing marks of moral difference between human beings, the people imitated by the arts must be represented either as 'better' than in real life, or as 'worse', or as they are. It is the same in fine art. Polygnotos idealised real life, Pauson caricatured it, Dionysios represented it faithfully. The same distinctions apply in every art-form. In literature, for example, Homer idealises human beings, Kleophon shows them as they are, the caricaturists Hegemon and Nikochares make them worse than in reality. A similar distinction marks off tragedy from comedy. Tragic characters idealise those of real life, comic characters parody them. (2)

A third difference is the manner in which each of these kinds of imitation can be made. If the things to be imitated and the means of imitation are the same, the author has two strategies: (1) narration, either in the first person throughout or, as Homer does, taking on different characters; (2) presenting the characters as if they live and move before our eyes. (3)

Content, method and style are the three areas of difference in artistic imitation. It follows that Sophocles, for example, is from one point of view an imitator of the same kind as Homer (in that both show 'higher' types of character), from another point of view of the same kind as Aristophanes (in that both show human action, people doing things). This is, some say, why 'drama' is so-called: it literally means 'something done'. (3)

The instinct for imitation is implanted in human beings from childhood. One difference between us and other animals is that we are the most imitative of living creatures. We learn our earliest lessons through imitation and take pleasure in all things imitated. Even things which are repugnant to us in real life, such as vermin or corpses, give us pleasure when reproduced with minute fidelity. The reason is that learning gives the liveliest pleasure, not only to philosophers but to people in general, even though their education is more limited. When we look at a picture, for example, our pleasure is in discovery and comparison. We may know the real-life subject, and can exclaim 'That's X to the life!' But even if we have never seen the original, we can take pleasure from the style, from the execution, the colours and things of that kind.

Imitation, then, is a natural human instinct. Another is our feeling for melody and rhythm (including poetic metre). This was the starting-point from which creators, at first by the light of nature and then with increasing skill, developed the art of literature. The art soon diverged, its direction depending on the character of each kind of author. 'Serious' authors, beginning with poems about the gods and high-achieving humans, represented 'fine' actions and 'higher' characters. Less 'serious' authors, beginning with lampoons, represented ordinary people. (4)

Tragedy is the imitation of an action, of the characters of those who do the action, and of their thought. By 'thought' I mean the faculty of expressing and then choosing between the options for action presented by each set of circumstances. In real life, politicians and trained rhetoricians (such as lawyers) do this. In old-fashioned tragedies authors made their characters speak like politicians; modern tragedians make their characters talk like rhetoricians. Just as the imitation of character reveals moral purpose in choosing or avoiding specific action (and if no action is chosen or avoided, no character is revealed), so thought is revealed when someone speaks for one side or other of an argument, or enunciates any informed opinion. (6)

The concept of *mimesis* is the heart of Aristotle's analysis of the aesthetics not merely of drama but of all the arts. Predictably, the word defies exact translation. It means setting up in someone's mind, by an act of artistic presentation, ideas that will lead that person to associate what is being presented with his or her previous experience. The pleasure we take in the arts is related to our cognitive faculty: recognition is a function of cognition. Our knowledge is reinforced and extended by what the arts reveal to us and in us; they extend our human experience and awareness, and make us more human.

Translations of *Poetics* variously render *mimesis* as 'imitation', 'representation' and 'simulation'. In philosophical terms, the difference between them is clear. A stick or a letter of the alphabet can be declared to be the 'representation' of a human figure but in absolute terms be nothing like it. An 'imitation' would be the drawing of a human figure, or one human deliberately pretending to be another: the intention is to remind the spectator of the person imitated. A 'simulation' starts from the same premise, but the likeness is more exact: the intention is to remove creative initiative from the spectator, to make him or her believe that the simulation *is* reality. Aristotle, talking of the arts, makes it clear that *mimesis*, for him, means 'imitation'. In his mind, a stick or letter of the alphabet could never 'imitate' (say) Oedipus, but only represent Oedipus in an abstract setting (for example, in a rhetorical discussion). A simulation of Oedipus would be identical to Oedipus in every respect, a clone. *Mimesis* requires similarity, but with difference enough to snag the spectator's mind, to draw him or her to participate in the experience that is the intention of the artwork. The arts consistently involve a three-way relationship: between artist, spectator and artwork. I create my sculpture, my music or my poem out of my own creative need, and also to relate to you; your response relates it to yourself and to me; complicity is established and essential. *Mimesis* requires that all art is ironical. No artwork exists in empty space; there is always an observer, and without an observer (even if that observer be the artist himself or herself) there is no art. This is particularly obvious in drama. The creator invites the spectator to become engaged with a performance, a *mimesis* of reality, and thence, if vicariously, with reality itself. A scientist, observing reality, need not become subjectively involved; the spectators of drama (which is not reality) are cajoled and manipulated into subjective involvement, willingly submit to it – and then, ironically, adjust and shape their involvement in ways that may or may not relate to the intentions of the playwright and performers.

In Greek tragedy, these ironies are layered and enhanced to an extent seldom paralleled in later theatre. Almost always, we are shown not simple 'action' (in the brute sense of Oedipus putting out his eyes or Klytemnestra butchering her husband in the bath-house), but the account of such action. Thus the usual actions of which we see *mimesis* are someone speaking and someone else listening. One effect of this is to focus attention less on what is being narrated than on the attitudes of the narrator and his or her audience – and often, what is said to 'frame' such moments makes us aware of the wider significance of what is being reported, a significance sometimes not appreciated by the characters on stage. Greek playwrights organized their material to provide opportunities not for physical deeds but for accounts of deeds and feelings. When physical deeds do take place on stage – examples are the suicides of Aias and Euadne in Sophocles' *Aias* and in Euripides' *Suppliants* respectively, the reading of crucial letters in Euripides' *Hippolytos* and *Iphigeneia in Tauris*, the jurors voting to condemn or acquit Orestes in Aeschylus' *Eumenides* and the nailing of Prometheus to the cliff-face in Aeschylus' *Prometheus Bound* – they are prepared, hedged about and followed by assertions of 'attitude' whose effect is to make the deed itself seem like the *mimesis* of a point of view, or a focusing of several points of view, rather than something that simply has its own existence.

In the same way, Greek playwrights establish a framework of emotion, intellectual attitude and character for each new person or point of view they present to us. Lines like 'Here comes Ismene, weeping for her sister. Her brow is dark, her face is red, tears stain her white cheeks like rain' (of Antigone's sister in Sophocles' *Antigone*) or 'Can't you stop her, Majesty? She's entranced. She'll be in the Greek camp, head over heels, before she knows it' (of the prophetess Kassandra in Euripides' *Women of Troy*) are typical. In every surviving play, the chief 'action' is a presentation of attitudes, either in monologue (lyrical or rhetorical) or in rapid, staccato conversation. Many plays – Aeschylus' *Suppliants* and *Prometheus Bound*, Sophocles' *Philoktetes* and Euripides' *Women of Troy* and *Herakles* are prime examples – consist almost entirely of such presentations, exploring every philosophical and emotional nuance of the characters and their situation; physical action is minimal.

A second characteristic feature of *mimesis* in Greek tragedy is the balance maintained between the extraordinary happenings and heightened emotions set up by the original myth-story, and the mundane style of their presentation. The Guard in Sophocles' *Antigone*, reporting the illegal burial of Polyneikes' body, is concerned as much with the stink of the corpse, the way he and his fellow-guards shut their eyes against the storm or squabbled about who should tell the ruler that his orders have been disobeyed, as with the almost supernatural nature of what they have witnessed. The Old Man in Sophocles' *Elektra* describes the chariot-race in which (he claims) Orestes has been killed with a wealth of detail about dust, snorting horses and cotter-pins. Medea in Euripides' play, about to commit the deed that is the goal and focus of the entire movement of the play till now, says matter-of-factly, 'What happens next is clear. I must kill the children quickly and escape from Corinth.' The servant's account, in Euripides' *Bacchae*, of the capture and dismembering of Pentheus is as full of bizarre and horrifying images, and as matter-of-factly told, as a Grimm folk tale. In our everyday lives, most of our words and actions are, precisely, mundane, while thoughts and feelings soar. The style of *mimesis* used in Greek tragedy applies that kind of ordinariness to amazing events and emblematic people, and the technique is one of the main contributors to the feeling of complicity so essential to dramatic form. When the opposite process happens in melodrama, when mundane events and people are given heightened presentation, we are moved to mock not weep; when Polyxena in Euripides' *Hecuba*, sacrificed on Achilles' tomb by the victorious Greeks, takes care to 'fall modestly, hide what no man should see', or the self-blinded Oedipus gropes to find, and hug, his small children at the end of Sophocles' *Oedipus Tyrannos*, our hearts are broken and our minds are challenged, all in a single moment. If this is what Aristotle means by 'purgation of the emotions of pity and terror by the arousal of those emotions', the nature of *mimesis* in Greek tragedy fulfils the role exactly.

THE CHARACTERS OF TRAGEDY

Heroes should be people of position and high renown: Oedipus, Thyestes, others of that rank. (13)

In respect of characters, there are four things to be aimed at. First, and most important, they must be 'good'. Speeches or actions which manifest moral purpose of any kind will express character, and if the purpose is 'good' the character will be 'good'. This is true whatever the status of the person. Even females can be 'good', although they are inferior to males; even slaves can be 'good', although they are beneath consideration.

The second thing to aim at is propriety. Valour is a male quality; for a female to show it is as inappropriate as would be revealing intellectual capacity.

Third, characters should be true to their 'reality' in the original myth. Hektor, for example, should not be shown as a coward, or Teiresias as a fool. This 'truth' is a different thing from the 'goodness' and 'propriety' described above.

Fourth, characters should be consistent within the drama. If the character is inconsistent in the original story, in the play that character should be consistently inconsistent.

I make my point by offering examples of works where these rules are not followed. In Euripides' *Orestes* Menelaos is, for no good reason, shown as less than 'good'. [Asked for help by his nephew Orestes, he refuses for expedient reasons.] In Timotheos' *Skylla*, Odysseus weeps, not nobly but from fear, in a manner both indecorous and inappropriate. Euripides' *Melanippe* offers another example of inappropriateness, when the female hero argues a philosophical point as if she were a man. In the same author's *Iphigeneia at Aulis*, the leading character displays inconsistency when her father Agamemnon threatens to sacrifice her: first she pleads for mercy and then she accepts her fate with a nobility and bravery which are entirely unprepared. (15)

In writing characters, as in organising the sequence of events, a playwright should always aim either at the necessary or the probable. When someone of a given character speaks or acts, their words or deeds should be inevitable or probable from what we know of them already. (15)

Since tragedy is an imitation of persons 'better' than average, dramatists should follow the example of good portrait painters, catching the essence of their sitters to be sure, but producing likenesses which are true to life and yet enhance it. Even when dramatists show characters who are irascible, indolent or have other faults, they should make them consistent and keep their dignity – as Agathon and Homer do in their portrayals of Achilles, showing him as both heroic and intemperate. (15)

Aristotle the philosopher deals here in absolutes, disregarding or rising above the fuzzy realities of both real life and drama. In the system of his science, ethics and social rank work like everything else, in a sequence of hierarchies. The qualities of each level in the hierarchy can be analysed and defined, and comparisons can be made between them. When this principle is applied to the writing of dramatic characters, the implications are manifold. Tragedy is a 'higher' art than comedy because it shows us characters who are 'better' than we are, not people like us or 'worse' than us. Tragic dramatists should show 'noble' characters; they should avoid putting people in situations or attributing to them behaviour or feelings inappropriate to their status. The plots of most tragedies show what happens to characters who choose, or are forced by circumstances, to reach beyond their status and to deny their nature.

The existence of hierarchy underpins Aristotle's dramatic theory in every particular, and comes directly from the Greek tragedians' decision (following Homer) to base their work on myth. (Even on the rare occasions when myth-stories are not used in the surviving plays, as in Aeschylus' *Persians*, dealing with the effects on the Persian state and its king Xerxes of their defeat by the Greeks at Salamis, the characters and events are selected and presented exactly as if they belonged to myth – a sharp ironical point in the case of *Persians*, whose original Athenian audience must have included many who had actually fought against the Persians at Salamis.) Myth also depends on hierarchies, and its stories concern the endless challenging and refraction of relationships, between beings of the same status and of different status. When god challenges god, god takes mortal form or a mortal aspires to the qualities and knowledge of the gods, myth is born. Aristotle points out in *Poetics* that the myth-cycles of a few regions – Argos, Thebes, Troy – were particular favourites with dramatists. But this was as much convention as a reflection of the 'undramatic' nature of other myths. As Aeschylus showed in *Suppliants* and *Prometheus Bound*, as Sophocles proved in *Aias*, as Euripides demonstrated in a dozen surviving plays, any myth and any crevice of any myth can inspire tragedy. Drama lies not in the events of the myth-stories themselves but in the spin a dramatist puts on them.

In the nature of things, myth is peopled with characters at the 'upper' end of Aristotle's hierarchies: gods, heroes, rulers, warriors, sages. Few myths centre, as folk tales do, on slaves or peasants – and if they do, such characters are usually 'higher' beings in disguise. Homer's epics and the surviving Athenian tragedies bustle with 'ordinary' people, but with a few exceptions – for example, the old nurses and advisers who have a long-standing, trusted relationship with their former charges: the range is from Odysseus' dignified nurse Eurykleia in Homer's *Odyssey* to the bawdy old woman in Euripides' *Hippolytos* who advises Phaidra to ease her longing for Hippolytos by seducing him, from Orestes' old tutor who recognizes him in Euripides' *Elektra* to the sage Teiresias in Sophocles' *Oedipus Tyrannos* – they seldom initiate action and their role is to comment on events, not change them. The same convention – that tragedy did not belong to 'ordinary' people – survived in Western drama well into the nineteenth century. The idea that 'little' lives can be filled with aspiration and disaster, which will evoke pity and terror in those to whom they are shown, was a discovery of eighteenth- and nineteenth-century novelists, and entered 'serious' drama later still. (Even then, most 'realistic' drama remained resolutely bourgeois. With a few notable exceptions, such as Büchner's *Woyzeck*, 1837, or Zola's *Thérèse Raquin*, 1873, working-class tragedy is an almost exclusively twentieth-century phenomenon.)

Anyone reading *Poetics* in the light of the surviving Greek tragedies will be struck by Aristotle's remarks that, even though women are 'inferior' to men, they can still be 'good', but that female characters should not be given 'manly' qualities, including intelligence. One of the glories of Greek tragedy is its range of female characters, drawn with a far greater variety, depth and psychological range than males. This richness may partly derive from the Greek view that the showing of emotion was a specifically 'womanly' thing, distinct from the dignity of bearing and consistency of attitude that were 'manly' attributes: drama generally thrives more on the presentation of emotion than on its avoidance. The variety and richness of female roles may reflect the excellence of travesty acting in the ancient theatre: it was one of the most important skills Greek actors learned. (There were no female actors.) It is possible that nowadays, influenced by centuries of psychological depth and resonance in the characters of tragedy, we respond more warmly to a Medea, say, or to an Elektra or a Hecuba than to a Prometheus or an Oedipus. Or it may simply be the challenge that such characters' dilemmas and characters offered to the dramatists: they certainly make the theatrical juices flow. Whatever the situation, Aristotle's remarks must make us wonder how ancient Greek audiences (mainly male) responded to such roles, whether they had different expectations from 'male' and 'female' plays, and if their reactions were like ours or different.

Aristotle's hierarchical theories impose on characterization a stiffness that is not always apparent in the plays themselves. He implies that characters are fixed, either in their true nature or out of it, and that the action of the play should either confirm them in what they are or show them changed by sudden 'reversal'. This is certainly true of some characters: examples range from Aeschylus' Prometheus and Xerxes to Sophocles' Oedipus and Elektra and Euripides' Medea and Hippolytos. Such characters are like onions: they are what they are, and their nature is gradually revealed, not changed, as skin after skin is removed from them. But the characters of other plays evolve before our eyes in a way not remarked on by Aristotle. Aeschylus' Orestes, for example, Sophocles' Philoktetes and Euripides' Ion (to take three roles more or less at random) grow and change before our eyes, are not psychologically the same by the end of the play as they were at the beginning. Other plays hinge less on individual identity than on kinship, not in the abrupt way of myth but with respect for the shifts and complexities of intimate relationships in real life. The relationship of Helen and her husband Menelaus in Euripides' *Helen* or that of Orestes and his sister Elektra in Aeschylus' *Libation-Bearers* show this in individuals. In *Women of Troy* and *Hecuba* Euripides examined the Trojan queen's relationships not only with her immediate family and the conquering Greeks but with her dying city and her people. Sophocles' *Antigone* is a cat's cradle of relationships, in which characters are impinged on by others, by the state and laws they live by, and by the authorities, mortal and fallible or divine and infallible, who moderate those laws.

A second major area in which Aristotle's schematic reasoning does not chime with the nuancing and insinuation so characteristic of dramatic method is the characterization of gods. Aristotle's metaphysical writings, following Plato, find an echo in the Judaeo-Christian notion that God is unique and unchanging, that the divine is by nature not devious. But absolutism of this kind was no part of the Greek dramatists' armoury. Taking their cue from Homer, who consistently invests the gods with human characteristics, they treated their immortal characters like any others, often deviating wildly from the original myth-stereotypes to do so. Aeschylus shows us a Titan (Prometheus) who snarls and rails at Zeus like a rock-bound Thersites, an Athene and Apollo who bicker like jealous mortal siblings, and a group of Furies howling and drooling with such nightmarish verisimilitude that (we are told) women went into labour and men rushed for the exits when they first appeared. The Herakles who appears *ex machina* at the end of Sophocles' *Philoktetes* is a no-nonsense non-commissioned officer, with far less presence (though far more actual authority) than the mortal Odysseus in the same play, and quite different from the suffering colossus depicted in Sophocles' *Women of Trachis* and Euripides' *Herakles' Children*, or the genial drunk who takes over the action in Euripides' *Alkestis*. Euripides' gallery of gods includes a sun-princess tormented because she chooses to take on mortal feelings (Medea), a devious and sexually ambivalent Dionysos (in *Bacchae*), and (in *Ion*) an Apollo whose immortal nature must be balanced against the fact that he is a cheat and rapist, so reluctant to face the mortals he has embroiled in his schemes that he refuses to appear in person, sending first his brother Hermes and then his sister Athene to speak for him. This kind of plurality, so bizarre to Christian readers and spectators of ancient drama, is absolutely consistent with the everyday Greek view that the gods were everywhere and could be anything they chose. It must have startled, intrigued, amused and edified the original audiences, but in a way entirely to do with popular entertainment and religious sentiment and foreign to the austerities of philosophy and metaphysical enquiry.

HAMARTIA

> The heroes' sufferings are caused less by innate wickedness than because of *hamartia*. (13)

Hamartia is one of three ideas in *Poetics* that were wildly misunderstood by Renaissance scholars. The misinterpretations then became canonical, so that subsequent theorizing about both Greek drama and drama in general, and a great deal of playwriting, drew on them in ways that Aristotle might have welcomed but would certainly not have recognized as his own.

Hamartia means 'error', no more and no less. Originally connected with spear-throwing (to mean missing or undershooting the target), it came to be used of any kind of mistake at all, from tripping over a stone to blurting out the wrong word or making a simple misunderstanding. In Greek philosophy, moral failing might be described as *hamartia*, in the sense that one 'falls short' of the ideal in thought or behaviour; but no Greek reader of the *Poetics* would have assumed such an exclusive usage here. If Aristotle had used *hamartia* to mean a moral flaw, it would have nullified his view that dramatic heroes should be morally 'good' (see page 20). The suffering of a 'bad' person might evoke in us not pity and terror but satisfaction.

The ancient Greeks, and the Olympian religion that

27

coloured all their thinking, held that balance and harmony, existed as a kind of all-encompassing universal state. Like everything else, it had a perfect form that was hard to discover or understand but to which aspiration was possible. Different classes of being had greater or lesser perception of this perfection. Gods understood more of it than mortals, human beings more than brute beasts, prophets more than ordinary people, aristocrats more than slaves. The changes and chances of existence were caused by deviations from perfection, upsetting the balance and disturbing the harmony, and to restore it these deviations had to be corrected. In particular, gods and mortals alike were connected by a web of relationships, individual to individual, family to family, group to group and state to state. When its mesh was torn, disharmony resulted.

Tears in the mesh, and the need to repair them, are the subject-matter of all Greek drama – and the hero's *hamartia* should be seen in light of this. The hero fails to maintain his or her place in universal harmony, and for balance to be restored that 'error' must be corrected. Sometimes the *hamartia* is wilful, arising perhaps from the *hubris* or arrogance that encourages mortals to equate themselves with gods, as Xerxes does in Aeschylus' *Persians* when he invades Greece, or Kreon does in Sophocles' *Antigone* when he puts his own laws above those of Zeus. But it might equally be inadvertent or the result of the actions of others. In Sophocles' *Women of Trachis* Herakles suffers as the result of the wickedness of Nessos (who plots to kill him) and the naivety of Deianeira (who is the unwitting agent of his agony). Eteokles in Aeschylus' *Seven Against Thebes* is destroyed not by his own fault but because his father lays a curse on him. Elektra, as represented in plays by all three surviving dramatists, is wholly innocent; indeed, her main action in the drama – encouraging Orestes to kill their mother – is a means of restoring harmony, not breaking it. Hecuba in Euripides' *Women of Troy* is a particularly interesting example. In myth, she tears the net of universal harmony by failing to heed a prophecy that her soon-to-be-born son Paris must be killed or he will grow up to topple Troy. She puts the maintenance of one part of the mesh (mother–son kinship) above another (Paris' place in the wider pattern of Fate). In his *Hecuba*, Euripides mentions this *hamartia* and allows us to draw the conclusion, if we wish, that it and its irresoluble nature are what lead to the suffering and madness Hecuba endures as the play proceeds. In *Women of Troy*, however, he is pursuing a different agenda entirely – warfare itself, and particularly the inhuman way victors treat the defeated, are what tear the net – and Hecuba is presented throughout as the dignified, sorrowing and entirely innocent victim of other people's actions.

This essentially animistic view of *hamartia*, as a kind of dropped stitch that must be gathered up if order is to be restored, is truly ancient Greek, essentially Aristotelian, and affects every character in every surviving play. In Aeschylus' *Prometheus Bound*, both Prometheus and Zeus disturb the balance, Prometheus by challenging the authority of the gods and Zeus by ignoring the decrees of Fate; restoration of order (which took place in the companion play, now lost) probably involved a change of heart by each of them. Apollo in Euripides' *Ion* has torn the net by allowing Kreousa and Ion to believe lies (that Kreousa's son is dead, that Ion is a foundling); harmony is restored only when they realize the truth (that Ion is Kreousa's son and Apollo is his father). Oedipus in Sophocles' *Oedipus Tyrannos*, often taken as the archetype of a hero whose moral *hamartia* arises from *hubris* ('he deliberately flouts Fate'), is actually innocent: he is blind to who he is, and harmony can be restored only when he finally understands. Euripides' *Bacchae* is a remarkable demonstration of *hamartia* of all kinds. Every mortal on stage misunderstands the nature and purpose of God, despite the fact that he is physically present, and active, to remind them.

The Renaissance hijacking of the discussion of *hamartia* by importing notions of moral guilt is the result of Christian, not pagan, thinking. And it leaves a gaping hole in the philosophy of every Greek tragedy to which it is applied. Christian ideas of guilt depend on the existence of a redeemer, a concept foreign to Greek thinking. In many Greek tragedies, God or the gods do appear and do restore order, but this is not redemption, it is more like parents intervening to end a children's squabble. The heroes of several tragedies – Oedipus in Sophocles' *Oedipus Tyrannos* and Aias in his *Aias* are egregious examples – bring about 'redemption' (in the sense of a restoration of harmony) by their own willed acts; others, such as Kreon in Sophocles' *Antigone* and Theseus in Euripides' *Hippolytos*, are 'punished' for wilful *hamratia* by the deaths of those closest to them, a tear in the universal pattern being repaired at the expense of innocent lives. Ideas of *hubris* leading to *hamratia* and thence to inevitable catastrophe may have an honoured place in post-Renaissance Western tragedies as diverse as *Macbeth*, *Phèdre*, *The Master Builder* and *The House of Bernarda Alba*, but they are foreign to ancient Athenian tragedy and absent from *Poetics*.

ANAGNORISIS AND *PERIPETEIA*

Anagnorisis ('recognition'), as the word suggests, is a change from ignorance to knowledge. Those destined by the writer for good or bad fortune recognise what has been hidden from them till now, that they are related or have long been enemies. The best kind of *anagnorisis* is coincident with *peripeteia*, as in Sophocles' *Oedipus Tyrannos* (see next paragraph). Obviously, other kinds of *anagnorisis* exist: those involving things of no importance, for example, or when we discover that someone has done or not done something. But the *anagnorisis* which is most intimately connected with plot and action is the one which happens between people. Combined with *peripeteia*, it produces either pity or terror, those elements we have defined as essential for tragedy.

The movement of a tragedy should involve a reversal (*peripeteia*) in the hero's circumstances, not from unhappiness to happiness but from happiness to unhappiness. It should arise not from wickedness but from *hamartia* in the hero.

Peripeteia should be subject always to the rules of probability or necessity. An example is the scene in Sophocles' *Oedipus Tyrannos* when the messenger from Corinth comes to hearten Oedipus and free him from his alarms about marrying his mother (whom Oedipus presumes to be Queen Merope), but by revealing whose son Oedipus actually is (that is, Queen Jokasta's) produces the opposite effect. In Theodektes' *Lynkeus* Lynkeus is led away to his death, and Danaos goes with him, meaning to slay him, but the logic of earlier parts of the story produces the outcome that Danaos is killed and Lynkeus saved. (11)

Aristotle's concepts of *anagnorisis* ('recognition') and *peripeteia* ('reversal') were as much misunderstood in Renaissance times as his view of *hamartia* – in fact, in a sequence following on from and building on the earlier misconception. In Renaissance thinking, *anagnorisis* involves the tragic hero suddenly being confronted with his or her own guilt, accepting it and bowing to the consequences – a paradigm of the Christian sacrament of confession. This acceptance in turn leads to *peripeteia*, the 180-degree turn in the hero's condition that is marked outwardly by physical suffering and inwardly by grace. From this point on, the dramatic progress may involve the hero in a headlong descent to humiliation and death, but the audience is presented with a double moral lesson, 'pity' arising from the details of this catastrophe and 'terror' resulting from our putting ourselves in the hero's place and identifying with his or her recognition and repentance.

This is coherent and fruitful as a way of writing tragedy, but its overtones of confession and penance have little to do either with ancient practice or with Aristotle. *Anagnorisis* in ancient tragedy takes two forms. The first is a simple admission that characters in the play recognize the truth when it is shown them, revealing an understanding of the universal pattern that they never had before. The plays are peppered with phrases like 'I understand at last' or 'I who was blind now see' or 'We hear and obey' – acceptance which is quite different from that of the Christian penitent,

32

in that it represents and enables a far more objective appraisal of the over-riding moral and ethical issues articulated in the play. *Anagnorisis* of this kind contains no moral imperatives whatever. Exactly the same denouement and the same response might result from another set of circumstances entirely, another tear in the fabric of universal harmony.

Anagnorisis of the more complex, Renaissance kind does occur, but extremely rarely and always in circumstances of deepest irony. An example – one of the finest dramatic scenes in all ancient tragedy – occurs in *Libation-Bearers*, the second part of Aeschylus' *Oresteia*. Part of the dramatic narrative of this play concerns the 'manning' of Orestes by the Chorus and Elektra, urging him to avenge his father's murder by killing his mother Klytemnestra, the murderer. In the scene itself, the climax of this process, Klytemnestra bears her breast to her son, saying 'I gave you my breast; I gave you life; can you strike me here, can you give me death?' At first sight her words seem like straightforward pleading to be spared. But Aeschylus has already set up an ironical context in which the murder is inevitable and Orestes has described himself as the 'serpent son that bites its mother's breast'. Orestes' realization of this is the final, essential step in the process of his 'manning'. In a clinching subtlety, Aeschylus leaves resonant in the air the question of how much Klytemnestra knows, how much her words involve an ironical assent in her own destiny.

Few other scenes in Athenian tragedy are similarly layered. Sophocles' *Oedipus Tyrannos*, for example, which plays such complex ironical games with the ideas of blindness and knowledge, contains none of them. Eurpides' most developed characters, Medea, Pentheus, Theseus in

33

Hippolytos, Hecuba, Elektra, even Helen and Menelaos in
Helen (the most teasingly ironical of all his extant plays), are
deprived of it. The standard *anagnorisis* in Greek tragedy is
simpler and blunter – so much so, in fact, that Aristotle in
Poetics simply lists the various types of recognition scene
and makes no comment:

There are six kinds.

(1) *Recognition by marks or objects.* This is the least
artistic – and also, from poverty of wit, the one most
commonly employed. Some marks are inherited (for
example the spear-shaped birthmark carried by all
descendants of the 'Sown Men', the mythical ancestors
of the Theban aristocracy), others are acquired after
birth (scars, for example, or ornaments such as neck-
laces). In Homer's *Odyssey*, when Odysseus returns
home disguised as a beggar, he is twice recognised by
the scar on his leg: once when his old nurse Eurykleia
recognises the scar when she washes him and once
when he baldly tells the swineherd Eumaios who he
really is and shows the scar to prove it. The first
recognition is more artistic because it happens by
accident, in the normal sequence of events, and not by
design.

(2) *Recognition contrived by the author.* This is arbitrary,
outside the logic of the events of the story, and is
therefore inartistic. In Euripides' *Iphigeneia in Tauris*
Iphigeneia's identity is revealed to her long-lost brother
Orestes logically in the letter scene. [She produces a
letter for him, thinking him far away in Argos, and begs
Pylades to deliver it.] But Orestes' identity is then baldly
announced, when Pylades hands him the letter – a

development which suits Euripides' purpose but is not inevitable from what has gone before.

(3) *Recognition by memory*. This is when a character sees or hears something which triggers recognition. In Dikaiogenes' *Cyprians* the disguised hero sees his dead father's picture and bursts into tears. In Homer's *Odyssey*, the stranger in Alkinoös' court is revealed as Odysseus when he weeps to hear the minstrel Demodokos singing of the Greeks who died at Troy.

(4) *Recognition by deduction*. In Aeschylus' *Libation-Bearers* Elektra says, in effect, 'Someone resembling me has come to weep at my father's tomb. No one resembles me except Orestes. Therefore Orestes has come.' In the play *Phineus' Children* a group of women are taken to the place where they were exposed as babies, and realise that the oracle was correct which prophesied their deaths. Of all types of recognition, this is the most artistic, second only to (6) below.

(5) *Recognition through false inference by the audience*. In the play *Odysseus Disguised* Odysseus says that he recognises a warbow we have no reason to believe that he has ever seen before – and we accept what he says as proof of his identity. [He comes to his own palace disguised as a beggar, and asks to compete against the suitors in the competition to string the great warbow from the armoury. In Homer, he reveals his true identity logically, by stringing the bow; in *Odysseus Disguised*, apparently – the play is lost – he announced that he recognised the bow as soon as he saw it, and everyone realised that he was Odysseus.]

(6) *Recognition arising logically from the incidents themselves*. Because this arises inevitably, needing no

signs, marks or other artificial aids, it is the most artistic kind of all. Examples are two of the recognitions described above: Oedipus' discovery of his true identity in Sophocles' *Oedipus Tyrannos* (it is perfectly natural that the Corinthian should want to allay his fears by telling him that Merope is not his real mother) and Orestes' discovery of Iphigeneia's identity in Euripides' *Iphigeneia in Tauris* (it is perfectly natural, in the circumstances, that she should want to send a letter). (16)

Peripeteia is similarly uncomplicated. So far from being the moral stage in a hero's self-knowledge that Renaissance and post-Renaissance critics claimed for it, it is a straightforward technical term. The dramatic narrative first shows us things one way and then changes them to something else. In one of his Occam's-razor-like definitions, Aristotle says that in comedy the *peripeteia* is from misery to happiness, in tragedy from happiness to misery. He goes on to qualify this, drawing a distinction between simple plots (centring on one person) and complex plots (centring on more than one), and pointing out the satisfaction of a plot in which *hamratia, anagnorisis* and *peripeteia* are bound up with one another to give the spectator the pleasures of constant surprise and of the knotting together of all the play's strands of both meaning and action. *Peripeteia* is not the moment when the moral roller-coaster of the play's action (embodied in what happens to the hero) reaches the height of its climb and begins its headlong fall; it is rather an objective phenomenon, the picking up of the dropped stitch in the web that is the outcome of the whole action – in Aristotle's own words, the *desis* ('binding-up') that follows *lusis* ('unravelling') to make the ideal dramatic sequence (see page 45).

MUTHOS

The importance of muthos. *Muthos*, the way the incidents of a play are structured, is the principal part of tragedy. Drama is an imitation not of people's appearance but of their actions and their lives. Just as, in life, moral qualities make us who we are but what we do determines the nature of our existence, so in plays the characters' moral qualities are subsumed in and secondary to their actions. The incidents of the play and their organisation are therefore all-important. You may string together a set of speeches expressive of character and well finished in point of diction and thought, but you will still not produce the essential tragic effect nearly so well as with a play which, however deficient in these respects, yet has a convincing sequence of incidents. *Muthos* is the first principle and soul of a tragedy, just as in fine art the clear chalk outline of a portrait will give more pleasure than even the most beautiful colours if they are laid on in haphazard and jumbled fashion.(6)

The word *muthos* is often baldly translated 'plot', but it means far more. If Aristotle had devoted over a third of the surviving *Poetics* to thoughts on plot alone, he would have been analysing melodrama, not tragedy. *Muthos* is material arranged to make a coherent and convincing artistic statement, and the word can apply to any art-form. A sculpture, a lyric poem or a piece of music can have *muthos* just as much as tragedy. In drama, *muthos* centres on what we would call 'plot' – that is, the sequence of events depicted – but it also embraces the editing of those events, the author's arrangement of material to draw out themes, make points and create effects. The three-way relationship, in the arts, between creator, artwork and audience allows all kinds of themes and overtones to exist through montage alone, without explicit statement. This is particularly the case in a performing medium, where the fact of presentation makes possible almost unlimited ironical layering.

We are more familiar, perhaps, with the use of the word *muthos* to describe this kind of montage in folk-lore and religion. Myths and stories formulated to express ideas about relationships, between individuals, within communities, bridging the gulf between the known and unknown worlds. By *mimesis* of the familiar, they offer us the opportunity to explore and come to terms with all kinds of inchoate ideas and emotions both within ourselves and in the world around us. The fact of *mimesis* creates an ironical distance between what is being presented and us, the observers, and this allows us to enter the experience on our own terms, to balance subjective feeling and objective assessment, to discover more about ourselves. The process is analogous to what happens in the arts – and it also gives due weight to entertainment, not the least reason for the existence of myths and arts alike.

Substance and magnitude. Anything beautiful, whether natural or made by human hands, must not only have an orderly arrangement of parts, but must also be of a certain magnitude. Beauty depends on suitable size no less than on order. A painting so tiny that we would scarcely be able to see it cannot be beautiful, any more than one so enormous (say a thousand kilometres long) that the eye cannot take it all in at once. In both cases, the unity and sense of the whole are lost on the spectator. And just as paintings need a magnitude which is both appropriate and easily comprehended, so too do works of literature.

Arbitrary lengths imposed on theatrical performances – for example by trying to fit a given number into a single festival day, parcelled out by the clock – have no part in artistic theory. The nature of the sequence of action depicted imposes its own boundaries: provided that everything in it is necessary and appropriate, it can be as long as it requires. As a rule of thumb, the right length is one in which the *muthos*, according to the law of probability or necessity, shows a change from bad fortune to good or from good to bad. (7)

Unity. Unity in dramatic organisation does not, as some people think, mean simply that the play has a single hero. Many things happen in an individual's life, and each individual does many things, which cannot be reduced to a single artistic unity. Just as, in the other imitative arts, unity of imitation means that a single subject is represented, in a work of literature the imitation should be of a single, unified sequence of actions, such that if any one of them is displaced or removed, the whole will be disjointed and disturbed. Any element which can be added or subtracted without making a visible difference is not an organic part of the whole. (8)

Universals and particulars. Writing fiction is about describing not actual, real events but events which are plausible or essential in certain given circumstances. It could be argued that fiction is a more philosophical and a higher art than factual writing, in that it tends to express the universal, factual writing the particular. By 'the universal' I mean how someone of a certain type will speak or act in a given situation, according to the laws of probability and necessity. Fiction does this even when it gives its characters the names of people who existed in real life. 'The particular', by constrast, is what real people – Alcibiades, for example – actually did or what was done to them. (9)

Simple and complex. Dramatic plots, like the sequences of action in real life of which they are an imitation, are either simple or complex. By 'simple' I mean a sequence of action in which logic and organic unity are present but which shows the change of fortune without reversal of the situation [*peripeteia*: see page 31] or recognition [*anagnorisis*: see page 31]. By 'complex' I mean a sequence in which the change is accompanied by such reversal, or by recognition, or by both. If they are present they should arise from the internal structure of the plot, in which every event is the necessary or probable result of what has preceded it. (There is a crucial difference between one thing happening merely *after* something else, and the same thing happening *because* of it.) (10)

Pity and terror. Pity and terror can be aroused by what we are shown on stage. But the better writers organise their works specifically to arouse such reactions, and this is to be preferred. Your tragic sequence of events should be so constructed that, even if someone merely hears it recounted and never sees it, he or she should thrill with horror and melt to pity at what takes place. This happens, for example, when we hear the story of Oedipus. To produce the effect by stage spectacle alone depends on the efforts of other people and is less artistic – and, since we should demand from an art-form not indiscriminate pleasure but only that which is proper to it, such proceedings lie outside the scope of tragedy. (14)

Choice of incidents. Since the task of the writer of tragedy is to arouse pity and terror by imitation, the potential for this must be inherent in the incidents being shown. Let us consider what the circumstances are which strike us as terrible or pitiful. Obviously, actions capable of this effect, like all other actions, must happen between persons who are either in sympathy with each other, not in sympathy or indifferent. If an enemy kills an enemy, there is nothing to excite pity either in the act or the intention – except so far as the suffering in itself is pitiful. So again with persons who are indifferent to one another. But when the tragic incident occurs between those who are near or dear to one another – if, for example, a brother kills or plans to kill a brother, a son his father, a mother her son, a son his mother, or any other deed of the kind is done or planned – these are events an author should prefer. (14)

The foundation of myth. No dramatist should change

the details of the basic myths – Klytemnestra should always be killed by Orestes – but writers may show invention of their own, using their skill to manipulate the traditional material. Let me explain more clearly what I mean. The central action must always happen: Medea, for example, must always kill her children. But it can be done in different ways and for different reasons. [Fifth-century] writers often made their characters do the action deliberately and with knowledge of all the facts (this is what happens in Euripides' *Medea*). An alternative is for the deed of horror to be done in ignorance, and the tie of kinship or friendship to be discovered afterwards. (In Sophocles' *Oedipus Tyrannos*, for example, Oedipus does not know that Laios is his father until long after he kills him.) A third alternative is to plan the deed in full knowledge, and then not do it. A fourth is to be about to do an irreparable deed in ignorance, and find out the truth before it is done. No other possibilities exist. The deed must either be done or not done, and these things must happen with our without knowledge.

Of all these ways, to be about to act in full knowledge, and then not to act, is the worst. It is shocking without being tragic, for no disaster follows. It is, therefore, only rarely found – as for example in Sophocles' *Antigone*, when Haimon threatens to kill his father Kreon and then draws back. Slightly better is that the deed should be done in ignorance of the full facts, as when Agaue in Euripides' *Bacchae*, in a maenad trance, mistakes her son Pentheus for a lion and tears him to pieces. There is then nothing cheap in this, and the discovery of the truth makes its full effect. The best is the kind of action in

42

Euripides' *Kresphontes,* where Merope, about to slay her son, recognizes at the last moment who he is and spares his life. A similar thing happens in Euripides' *Iphigeneia in Tauris,* where a sister recognises her brother just as she is about to kill him. These considerations are one reason why only a few myth-families furnish subjects for tragedy. Having discovered by experiment the right kind of subjects to produce the true tragic effect, authors are compelled to have recourse to those houses whose history contains incidents like these. (14)

No Greek tragedy is simply about what its events depict. Each carries an enormous weight of assertion, nuance, implication and suggestion, both intellectual and emotional, drawing strength equally from the predispositions of author and spectator. Some of these overtones are apparent: no one, for example, would assume that Euripides' *Medea* was simply about a wronged wife who kills her children. But in other cases the nuancing is so delicate that it can escape notice altogether. What, for example, did ancient Athenian audiences think about the attitudes to war implicit in Aeschylus' *Persians* or Euripides' *Women of Troy*? Can those feelings ever be replicated in audiences more familiar with (say) Auschwitz or Hiroshima than with the battle of Salamis or the Melian affair? The gulf is particularly striking when we use the loaded term 'religious drama' to describe Greek tragedy. Modern European views about the natures of God and of religious practice have for centuries been projected, subconsciously but forcefully, on to the ancient plays, so that the resonances that ancient writers and their audiences might have heard, unspoken, in (say) Aeschylus' *Oresteia*, Sophocles' *Oedipus at Kolonos* or Euripides' *Ion* have been all but drowned.

Organising the muthos. Whether authors use pre-existing stories or invent their own, they should first sketch the general outline and then fill in the episodes and amplify in detail. What I mean by 'general outline' can be illustrated by the story of Iphigeneia in Tauris. A young girl is sacrificed, disappears mysteriously from the eyes of those who sacrificed her and is transported to another country where the custom is to offer up all strangers to the goddess. To this ministry she is appointed. Some time later her own brother chances to arrive. (The fact that Apollo's oracle for some reason ordered him to go there, and the purpose of his coming, lie outside the general plan of the play.) He comes, is seized and is about to be sacrificed when he reveals who he is. The mode of recognition may be either that used in Euripides' play (where the sister asks her brother's friend to deliver him a letter – and he does so before her eyes) or in Polyeidos' play (in which the brother exclaims, as anyone might in these circumstances, 'So it was not my sister only, but I too, who was doomed to be sacrificed', and by that remark is saved). This is the outline. The author now fills in the names and fleshes out the episodes. These must be relevant to the action. In the story of Iphigeneia and Orestes, for example, there is the fit of madness which led to Orestes' capture, and his and Iphigeneia's escape from Tauris by the trick of pretending to take the goddess' statue to the beach to be purified.

In plays, episodes are few and short. In epic poems, by

contrast, they bulk out the entire artwork. The story of Homer's *Odyssey*, for example, can be stated briefly thus: A certain man is absent from home for many years, is tormented by Poseidon and left desolate. Meanwhile his home is in a wretched plight – suitors of his wife are wasting his substance and plotting against his son. At length, tempest-tossed, he himself arrives, makes certain persons acquainted with him, attacks the suitors and is himself preserved while he destroys them. This is the essence of the *muthos*; the rest is episode. (17)

Desis *and* lusis. Every tragedy falls into two parts, complication (*desis*) and unravelling or denouement (*lusis*). Incidents extraneous to the action are frequently combined with a portion of the action proper, to form the *desis*; the rest is the *lusis*. By *desis* I mean everything from the beginning of the *muthos* to the part which marks the turning point to good or bad fortune. *Lusis* is everything from the beginning of the change to the end.

In any *muthos*, in order that overall artistic unity be preserved, *lusis* should follow logically from *desis*. (18)

Aristotle's remarks about *muthos* are almost entirely practical. He talks of coherence, appositeness, complication, denouement and a dozen such matters with a blend of critical pungency and the over-enthusiasm of the amateur. (No professional playwright needs to be told, for example, to visualize or to be reminded that characters extraneous to the main action need to be carefully inserted.) He says nothing at all explicit about the style of *muthos* used by each of the great tragedians – a matter for regret, given the acuity of his comments on Homer's methods in the *Iliad* and *Odyssey*. We are further disadvantaged by the scantiness of evidence. Less than twenty per cent of Euripides' work survives, less than five per cent of Aeschylus', less even than that of Sophocles, a handful of lines from other writers. There is little consistency of approach between the surviving works, even those by the same playwrights. To attempt a theory of Greek tragedy today, based on surviving evidence, would be an act of creation, not analysis.

With the exception of *Persians*, all Aeschylus' surviving works are torsos: even the *Oresteia* lacks its final portion, the comic, pastoral satyr-play that would have rounded off its sequence in the ancient theatre. *Seven Against Thebes* and *Suppliants* are thought to have been parts of four-play sequences, *Prometheus Bound* half of a two-play sequence. All that can safely be said about Aeschylus' *muthos* is that in the surviving works he uses the Chorus to present a kind of wider panorama of relevance and meaning, and then narrows the focus on to specific characters and specific, emblematic scenes. The general is constantly refracted through the particular, and vice versa, in a way that is unique to Aeschylus in ancient drama and that some commentators have likened less to play-writing than to the articulation of themes and ideas in such classical-music composers as Bach or Beethoven. The process can be demonstrated in the opening scenes of *Agamemnon* (first play in the *Oresteia* sequence). Something like two-thirds of this sequence is given to the Chorus, who tell us about the Trojan War, how the Greek leader Agamemnon sacrificed his own daughter to bring fair winds for the fleet, and how that sacrifice imposed an ancient family curse on one more generation. In between all this, individual actors, in two short scenes, give specific focus to the general choral uneasiness: the Watchman anxiously wonders what Agamemnon will find on his return from Troy, and the king's wife Klytemnestra announces the welcome for her husband that we know will end in his death. Aeschylus' other surviving plays, with the exception of *Prometheus Bound* (which focuses throughout on individuals), use a similar kind of *muthos* – and all are alike also in that we are given no glimpse of Aeschylus' own views, the authorial voice is impossible to identify. In both respects, Aeschylus seems closer to Homer than to either Sophocles or Euripides, but the evidence is too scanty to be dogmatic.

Sophocles is the most elusive of the three surviving tragedians. In nineteenth-century classical scholarship he was the most admired, partly because of the elegance of his language (his choruses are some of the finest of all extant Greek poetry) and partly because two of his plays, *Oedipus Tyrannos* and *Antigone*, seemed to offer not only entertainment but moral and philosophical edification that chimed with the spirit of the times. Unlike those of Aeschylus, his surviving plays maintain close focus throughout. Scenes follow one another lucidly and logically, like beads on a string, and the choruses (which are similarly self-contained) add new ideas and sentiments to the ongoing argument without disturbing or redirecting the dramatic flow, as Aeschylus' and Euripides' choruses so often do. 'Argument' used to be a key concept in Sophoclean criticism, each play being claimed to examine a specific philosophical idea (the nature of law in *Antigone*, of leadership in *Aias*, of personal loyalty and political necessity in *Philoktetes*) and to reach a conclusion that left no doubt about what Sophocles wanted

his audience to believe. For nineteenth-century peda-
gogues, this didactic closure was one of the most appealing
features of his work. Furthermore, Aristotle's frequent
references to *Oedipus Tyrannos* in *Poetics* led people to
believe that it was the very paradigm of how Greek tragedy
should be written, and that all other works should be
judged against it – in many cases, to their detriment. The
view is nonsense. *Oedipus Tyrannos* is a masterpiece, but its
muthos is unique even in Sophocles' surviving work.
Antigone is superficially similar, but each of the other plays
is *sui generis*. *Oedipus at Kolonos* blends mystical poetry with
rapid, even melodramatic physical action. *Elektra* and *Aias*
are powerful psychological studies of characters in emotional *extremis*; their nearest equivalents are Euripides'
Medea and *Hecuba* respectively. Physical action in *Philoktetes*
is almost non-existent, dramatic tension and energy coming from the exploration of individual characters and the
interplay between them.

At first glance, Euripides' style in the surviving plays
seems more varied and experimental than the work of
either of his colleagues. He writes dialectical drama (*Suppliants*), case-studies of individuals (*Herakles*) and of whole
societies in turmoil (*Women of Troy*, *Orestes*), adventure
stories (*Iphigeneia in Tauris*), meditations on identity
(*Helen*), love (*Alkestis*), the nature of God (*Ion*, *Bacchae*),
'didactic' tragedy of Sophoclean intensity (*Hippolytos*), even
– in *Elektra* – a play that seems the very template for a 'well-
made' Greek tragedy. This disparity of style is matched by
dazzling technical variety: he finds a new *muthos*, often
unexpected but always appropriate and satisfying, for
whatever kind of play he writes. In all his surviving plays,
however (with the exception of *Rhesos*, a straightforward

dramatization of part of Homer's *Iliad*), he blurs the distinction between choral scenes and scenes with actors, dividing the musical interest, sharing the emotional and dialectical energy until each play is a single, if kaleidoscopic, experience. His tone, throughout his extant work, is sharply ironical and sceptical – so much so that it seems, rightly or wrongly, to be his own authorial voice and people have identified in it a response to his real situation, the dying years of the Glory that was Athens.

Throughout *Poetics* as it survives, Aristotle's remarks on style, comparing one dramatist with another, are infrequent and throwaway, as if his views were already too well known to need rehearsing or the question were irrelevant to his argument. He seems to prefer fifth-century writers to those of his own day, Sophocles and Euripides to their contemporaries, Sophocles to Euripides. (He is sparing in his comments on Aeschylus, and effusive about Homer.) In all this, there is little of what a modern literary critic might recognize as a systematic response, and our understanding is further hampered by the small number of actual surviving plays: three dozen tragedies out of the hundreds, possibly well over a thousand, to which Aristotle and his researchers had access. To the modern eye, the surviving plays suggest a variety of approach and a suppleness of response to the challenges of the medium that Aristotle's generalities fail to address; his comments on *muthos* show this lack of rigour to a particularly marked degree. But scarcity of evidence makes all such judgements tendentious: perhaps Aristotle's comments addressed standard practice, and achievement, in ways we can never now recapture.

TRAGEDY AND EPIC POETRY

Epic is poetic imitation in verse but describing events rather than showing them. Like tragedy, it should be organised on dramatic principles. It should have for its subject a single sequence of events, complete and of substance, with a beginning, a middle and an end. It will thus satisfy because of its own organic unity, as if it were a living organism. It will differ in structure from other forms of narrative, such as history, which by its nature deals not with a single sequence of events but with a period of time, including everything that happened within that period to individuals and to groups of people, little connected together as the events may be. For example, there were sea-battles [in 480 BC] against the Persians at Salamis and against the Carthaginians in Sicily, but their only connection is chronological.

Although most writers of epic are aware of this, Homer once again surpasses all others. Although the Trojan War had a beginning and an end, he makes no attempt to cover it entirely in his *Iliad*. It would have been either too vast to take in at all, or, if he had kept it within moderate limits, too crammed with incidents. As it is, he concentrates on a single portion, the events which led Achilles first to withdraw from and then return to the fighting, and the death and ransoming of Hektor, and enriches and varies it by referring to other events outside this sequence, for example when he lists all the Greek states who sent ships and men to Troy. Other writers of epic, even if they centre on a single hero, a single period, or a single sequence of events, keep digressing to tell other stories. The result is that the *Iliad* furnishes the plot for a single tragedy, or at most two; likewise the *Odyssey*; the *Minor Iliad*, by contrast, for no less than eight: the quarrel over Achilles' armour, the stories of Philoktetes, Neoptolemos and Eurypylos, Odysseus' entering Troy disguised as a beggar, the Fall of Troy, the story of the Women of Troy, the Departure of the Fleet. [The *Minor Iliad*, now lost, is remembered chiefly as the inspiration for half a dozen surviving tragedies, on themes listed here.] (23)

Epic, like tragedy, should be simple or complex, and should be based on character or suffering. With the exception of music and spectacle, its components are the same (for example it includes *anagnorisis*, *peripeteia* and scenes of lyrical grief), and its thought and language must be elevated. In all these respects Homer is our earliest and finest model. Each of his epics has a double structure. The *Iliad* has a simple *muthos* [see page 40] and deals with suffering; the *Odyssey* has a complex *muthos* filled with recognition scenes, and deals with character. In diction and thought they are equal, and supreme. (23)

Epic differs from tragedy in the scale on which it is constructed, and in its metre. As regards scale or length, I have already suggested that the beginning and the end must be capable of being brought within a single experience – implying something shorter than Homer's poems, more like the four plays performed on a single day at a dramatic festival. [That is, some 5,000–6,000 lines of verse. The *Iliad* and *Odyssey* are each three times as long. By comparison, *King Lear* contains some 3,200 lines.] Epic poetry has, however, a great – a unique – capacity for enlarging its dimensions. In tragedy we cannot imitate several different events which happen at the same time. We are limited to the events being enacted at any given moment by actors on the stage. In epic, by contrast, owing to the narrative form, many events simultaneously transacted can be presented, and so long as these are relevant to the subject, they add mass and dignity to the poem. This advantage gives epic both grandeur of effect and diverting variety. As many writers of tragedy have found to their cost, sameness of incident can soon produce satiety.

Another admirable quality in Homer is his certainty about how much to intrude his own authorial self in his work. Writers of fiction should speak as little as possible in the first person: this hinders imitation. Some writers constantly put themselves on stage, imitating but little and rarely. Homer, after a few prefatory words in the first person, at once brings in a man, woman or other personage, such as a god – and supplies each of them with character.

The amazing is an essential ingredient of fiction – and epic, because its events are described and not presented by actors, offers it more scope. Achilles' pursuit of Hektor, three times round the walls of Troy, would be ludicrous on stage, the Greeks standing still and taking no part, Achilles waving them out of the way. In an epic poem such absurdity is not a feature. Everyone enjoys being amazed: this may be inferred from the fact that everyone who tells an anecdote embroiders it, knowing that this will please the hearers. Homer shows other writers of fiction how to tell lies skilfully. (24)

Writers should prefer what is impossible but plausible to things which are possible but implausible. The implausible should, if possible, be excluded, and if this is impossible it should be kept out of the main action of the story (an example is Oedipus' ignorance, in Sophocles' *Oedipus Tyrannos*, of how his father died). It should not be made essential to the story, like the false story told of Orestes' death in a chariot race in Sophocles' *Elektra*. [The messenger claims that Orestes died at the Pythian Games, which did not at that time exist.] The plea that otherwise the plot would have been ruined is ridiculous; such a plot should not in the first instance be constructed. In this respect, even Homer nods: an example is the passage in his *Odyssey* when Odysseus is landed in Ithaka while still asleep. How intolerable such a scene would be if an inferior poet had invented it! As it is, only the poetic charm with which Homer invests the scene veils its implausibility (24)

Fine language should be kept for moments in the work where action, character and argument are not presented. These things are obscured, not revealed, by a style that is overbrilliant. (24)

People sometimes ask which is the higher form of imitation, epic or tragedy. The argument against drama is as follows. If by 'higher' we mean more refined and if by 'more refined' we mean that which appeals to the discriminating, then the current kind of drama, imitating anything and everything, is manifestly most unrefined. Audiences today are supposed to be too dull to follow what is happening unless the performers grossly overact, the musicians writhe and twirl as if they are imitating discus-throwers or pull the leading dancer here and there as if he were Odysseus and they were [the many-headed sea-monster] Skylla. Actors of the older generation looked down on their successors – Aeschylus' actor Mynniskos used to call Kallippides and Pindaros 'monkeys' because of the way they threw themselves about. Drama, generally, stands to epic as those younger actors stood to their elders. Epic is addressed to a cultured audience who need no acting-out, drama to those who do and are therefore less discriminating. Case proved: it is the lower of the two.

The argument for drama is as follows. The criticisms above apply to performance, not composition. Performers of epic can wave their arms just as much as actors – remember Sosistratos or Mnasitheus the Opuntian. Not all physical action is to be condemned, but only that of bad performers. In any case, tragedy, like epic, can produce its effect even without being acted, when it is merely read. Vulgarity of performance is not inherent.

Drama is superior because it contains all the elements of epic, and adds music and stage-show as important accessories. Put together, these produce the most intense of artistic pleasure. Its vividness is as apparent when it is read as when it is acted. It attains its end more economically – and a concentrated effect is always more pleasurable than one which is spread over a long time and so diluted. What, for example, would *Oedipus*

Tyrannos be like if it were as long as the *Iliad*? Epic imitation has less unity: one epic will provide material for several tragedies. If the story adopted by a writer of epic has strict unity, it must either be concisely told and appear truncated, or, if it conforms to the epic canon of length, it must seem weak and watery.

If, then, tragedy is superior to epic in all these respects, and moreover, fulfils its specific function better as an art – for each art, as I have already stated, ought to produce not random pleasure but the pleasure proper to it – it plainly follows that tragedy, since it attains its end more perfectly, is the higher art. (26)

THE UNITIES

Unity of action (tragedy). Unity [of action] does not, as some people think, mean simply that the play has a single hero. Many things happen in an individual's life, and each individual does many things, which cannot be reduced to a single artistic unity. (8)

Unity of action (epic). Homer never attempts to make the whole Trojan War the subject of his *Iliad*, though that war had a beginning and an end. It would have been too vast a theme, and not easily embraced in a single view. If, again, he had kept it within moderate limits, it must have been overcomplicated by the variety of the incidents. As it is, he detaches a single portion, and admits as episodes many events from the general story of the war – such as the catalogue of the ships and others – thus diversifying the poem. All other poets take a single hero, a single period, or an action single, indeed, but with a multiplicity of parts. (23)

Unity of imitation. As in the other imitative arts, unity of imitation means that the imitation should be of a single, unified sequence of actions, such that, if any one of them is displaced or removed, the whole will be disjointed and disturbed. (8)

Unity of time. The nature of the sequence of action depicted imposes its own boundaries. Provided that everything in it is necessary and appropriate, it can be as long as it requires. (7)

So far as possible, tragedy endeavours to confine itself to a single revolution of the sun, or but slightly to exceed this limit; whereas the sequence of action depicted in epic has no limits of time. (5)

Writing in 1570, the Italian theorist Lodovico Castelvetro (1505–71) elaborated the above remarks into the theory of the Three Unities (of time, place and action). This was almost immediately assumed to be a creation of Aristotle himself. It was taken as prescriptive by drama theorists and those playwrights who modelled their works on what they took to be the practice of ancient Greece. The theory states, in essence, that a play should take place over a single, consecutive period of time in a single location, and should deal with a unified group of people taking part in a single sequence of action.

For Aristotle, unity of action was a matter of logic, the organization of the apposite. It was achieved by an author's selection and presentation of material, and embodied that author's 'spin' on the story told. It was not implicit in the material, but revealed the intellectual qualities of the writer. One sign of a bad writer was that material was selected and presented in a random-seeming or arbitrary fashion; one sign of a good writer was that all material used was made to seem essential – even in cases, like those he quotes from Homer or Euripides, where it is not.

Unity of time was a function of this organic cohesion. It hardly mattered whether the time-span imitated was a few hours (the 'single revolution of the sun' Aristotle mentions) or much longer, so long as it encompassed a single unified action. Time in the surviving tragedies is elastic. Some (Sophocles' plays in particular) show events happening in a short span, in which the illusion is created that 'real' time and 'dramatic' time are the same. (But questions remain. How long, in 'real' time, did it take Odysseus and Neoptolemos to convince Philoktetes to return to Troy? Did Aias' suicide follow as fast on the heels of his leaving Tekmessa as the play makes it seem?) Aeschylus' plays, many of them written as parts of longer units, collapse and expand time to suit the psychological narrative – he is a master of slowing down or accelerating the speed of the action to articulate wider themes and allow opportunities for multiple poetic and philosophical resonance. Many of Euripides' surviving plays, while seeming to take account of the 24-hour 'rule', in fact work conjuring tricks with time. The women of Thebes go off to Mount Kithairon in *Bacchae*, and ten minutes later (in elapsed stage time) a cowherd returns to give details of their 'orgies' there; similarly, Pentheus exits to spy on them, and one chorus later the Messenger is on stage with a detailed account of the king's journey up the mountain, his spying, capture and execution. In *Suppliants* Theseus announces that he will send soldiers to Thebes to demand the bodies of the dead heroes; half a page later the soldiers have reached Thebes (a journey of some 150 km), the argument has been held and won, the soldiers have returned, the funeral pyres are built, lit and blazing, and the bodies have been brought. As with everything else in drama, *mimesis* of time passing is a subtle and deceptive skill, organized often to procure what the critic Kenneth Burke once called 'perspective by incongruity'.

The unity of place, invented by Castelvetro and enthusiastically supported by later scholars, is a creation of the theatre of illusion of modern times, not of ancient drama. Many surviving Greek plays do take place in a single location (usually an open space before an imposing gateway), but others do not. Some scholars, not used to theatre practice, have deduced that in the absence of painted scenery it was physically possible to show only a single location in the Greek theatre, and that the unity of place was observed for practical as well as philosophical reasons. A moment's reflection on Shakespeare's plays from a later age, on such Greek tragedies as Sophocles' *Aias* (where the scene changes halfway through the action from an encampment to a beach by a forest) or on the multiple locations of some Aristophanes comedies, should have shown that this was nonsense. If a character comes on and announces 'We're in the Greek camp' or 'This is the Palace Gate of Mycenae' or 'Here flows the Nile', that is all the scene-painting we need – and such indications can be provided as often as required, consistent with the play's overall unity and logic. We are not embarrassed by the shifting of the locations of, say, *Richard II* from court to monastery to jousting-ground to the great hall of parliament to castle garden, or by the switch, in Aristophanes' *Clouds*, from Strepsiades' bedroom to the street outside to the interior of Socrates' Thinkery. Why should ancient tragedy be different or cause us more anxiety? Of all the things imitated in ancient drama, location is the most instantly established, the most fluid and the easiest to change.

Thus much may suffice concerning tragedy and epic in general, their respective kinds and parts and the differences between them, and the causes that make a work good or bad. (26)

RECOMMENDED BOOKS

The Penguin Classics translation of *Poetics* by Malcolm Heath (Viking, London, 1996) is lucid and has an exceptionally good introduction and notes. Stephen Halliwell, *Aristotle's Poetics* (Duckworth, London, 1986) is a scholarly study, heavy reading but worthwhile. A.O. Rorty (ed.), *Aristotle on Tragic and Comic Mimesis* (Scholar Press, Aldershot, 1992) is a collection of stimulating critical essays. The most recommendable translations of extant Greek tragedy are in the Chicago Press series (American accented) and the Methuen Greek Drama Series (English accented). Of the many studies of Greek tragedy by modern classical scholars, H.D.F. Kitto, *Greek Tragedy* (Methuen, London, third edition, 1961) is particularly recommended to non-specialists.